WE MOURN

CHIEF

FALLEN.

ABRAHAM LINCOLN
COMES HOME

Robert Burleigh ★ paintings by Wendell Minor

HENRY HOLT AND COMPANY
New York

To the Eash family: Joan, Marcia, Kay, and Tim
(And in memory of Gary)
—R. B.

To my friend and fellow artist Doug Marlette (1949–2007)
—W. M.

The illustrator wishes to thank Professor Wayne Wesolowski for making his scale model of the steam engine *Nashville* and Lincoln's funeral car available as reference for the illustrations in this book. The train is in the permanent collection of the Abraham Lincoln Presidential Library and Museum in Springfield, Illinois. A special thanks is due to Director Thomas E. Schwartz, PhD, for his permission to photograph the model for such use. The resources of the Abraham Lincoln Book Store of Chicago and its owner, Daniel R. Weinberg, were extremely helpful in finding additional written and visual material relating to Lincoln's funeral train. (As many as forty-two different engines were used to bring President Lincoln's body home to Springfield. The engine depicted in this book is the *Nashville*, perhaps the grandest of them all. Locomotive Number 58 of the Chicago & Alton Railroad had the honor of taking the president's funeral car the last 185 miles of its journey.)

The flag shown on the endpapers is an original image, one of many printed as small paper flags that served as popular symbols of mourning during Lincoln's funeral observances.

For further information about Lincoln and the funeral train, the following books will be helpful:
The Lincoln Funeral Train by Scott D. Trostel (Camtech Publishing, 2002);
The Lincoln Train Is Coming by Wayne and Mary Cay Wesolowski (published independently, 1995);
Lincoln's Assassins: Their Trial and Execution by James L. Swanson and Daniel R. Weinberg (Arena Editions, 2001);
Lincoln's Photographs: A Complete Album by Lloyd Ostendorf (Rockwood Press, 1998);
The Abraham Lincoln Presidential Library and Museum, www.alplm.org.

Henry Holt and Company, LLC
Publishers since 1866
175 Fifth Avenue
New York, New York 10010

Henry Holt® is a registered trademark of Henry Holt and Company, LLC.
Text copyright © 2008 by Robert Burleigh
Illustrations copyright © 2008 by Wendell Minor
All rights reserved.

ISBN-13: 978-0-8050-7529-8

Book designed by Laurent Linn
The artist used gouache watercolor on Strathmore 500 Bristol paper to create the illustrations for this book.
Printed in Mexico

ABRAHAM LINCOLN
COMES HOME

The buggy rumbled past the barn and through the rusty gate. A single lantern dangled from the near side of the horse's harness. The lantern cast shadows that rose and fell with each bounce.

Luke's father flipped
the reins and called to the
horse in a soft voice.
Luke lurched sideways
as the buggy crossed over
the old wood bridge. It was
so dark he could hardly tell
where the land ended and
the sky began.

The road stretched out. Where was the train now? Luke half drowsed to the steady rhythm of hooves on the hard dirt. The train tracks were still miles away, next to Hardin's Mill.

Luke loved trains. Trains took you places. (One day, his father said, they would take a train to Washington to see the president's house!) Tonight's train, though, was different. It carried the body of Abraham Lincoln.

The boy thought of the dead president, with his sad face. Some folks said it was the saddest face they had ever seen. But Luke knew if he could have talked to Abe Lincoln he would have liked him.

The buggy eased to a halt. Luke
breathed a smell of metal mixed with
the faint scent of lilacs. He climbed
down and stood with his father close
to the iron rails.

Bonfires blazed.
Others were here,
too, waiting for the
funeral train. Yes,
the train was coming.
Somewhere the
wheels were turning,
turning.

How far it had come! Day after day, night
into morning. Past cities and towns with tolling
bells. Past speeches and silence. Past black
drapes, heaped roses, archways of green leaves,
and the sound of muffled drums.

Luke squinted. There! A tiny flicker was moving very slowly across a field.

Up and down the track torches flared—swoosh, swoosh—like giant fireflies. Surprised by the brightness, horses whinnied and stamped.

The train rattled into view. A clapper clanged. The engine grew immense.

Luke could see Abe Lincoln's picture above the cowcatcher. He felt the ground shiver under his feet.

He glanced up at his father. In the eerie orange glow, tears were streaming down his father's cheeks. Luke had never seen his father cry before.

Engulfed in the harsh roar of iron on iron, Luke counted the cars one by one.

The coffin was in the next-to-last car. The windows were so dark. Luke stood on his tiptoes and raised his arm and waved.

The noise faded. The prairie swallowed
the *clack-clack-click*, all the way to nothing.
An owl hooted. Suddenly a lone voice
shattered the stillness. . . .

"You're coming home, Abraham Lincoln.
Home at last."
For a long time no one stirred. No one
spoke. Then it was over.

A thin line of light rested on the distant horizon. Luke hoisted himself onto the buggy's sideboard and tumbled in.

In the cool air he snuggled against his father's warm shoulder. He was tired now. The sound of the buggy wheels made him think of train wheels, still turning. It was the last thing he remembered before he fell asleep.

AFTERWORD

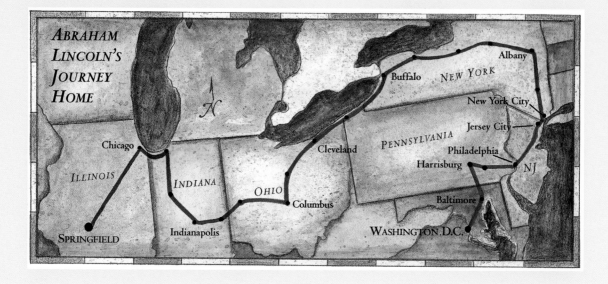

ABRAHAM LINCOLN was shot by John Wilkes Booth in Ford's Theatre, Washington, D.C., on April 14, 1865, and died the following morning. It was just a week after the end of the Civil War.

Lincoln's wife, Mary Todd Lincoln, decided that the president should be buried in Springfield, Illinois, where Lincoln had lived as an adult and had gained recognition as a political leader.

After funeral services in Washington, Lincoln's body was taken by train to Springfield. The train—roughly following the route Lincoln had taken on coming to Washington in 1861—stopped for additional funeral services in other northern cities. The total journey took thirteen days.

Millions of people passed by the dead president's casket or watched as huge processions walked behind the hearse through city streets. The funeral train was greeted by many more mourners in hundreds of small towns.

Wherever the slow-moving train passed—rain or shine, day or night—people gathered by the tracks to pay their final respects. One historian said it was "the mightiest outpouring of national grief the world had yet seen."

A few years before his death, Lincoln told his wife that he wished to be buried "in some quiet place." He was buried on May 4, 1865, on a grassy hill in Oak Ridge Cemetery in Springfield.

INTERESTING FACTS ABOUT
THE LINCOLN FUNERAL TRAIN

★ Abraham Lincoln's funeral train traveled over 1,600 miles on its route from Washington, D.C., to Springfield, Illinois.

★ About thirty million people attended religious services, watched the funeral procession in various cities, or watched the train pass.

★ In all, twelve funerals were held along the way, and about a million people walked past the open casket.

★ At the first funeral, in Washington, D.C., General Ulysses S. Grant sat alone in front of the coffin, weeping. He called it "the saddest day of my life."

★ Among the forty thousand marchers at the funeral procession in Washington were many crippled soldiers on crutches, along with four thousand African-American Union soldiers, all in lines of forty straight across.

★ The funeral train's engines (there were several used along the way) were draped in black and had a large photograph of Lincoln in front.

★ The body of Lincoln's favorite son, Willie, who had died in 1862, was removed from its burial place and taken in the same car as his father to be buried in Springfield.

★ Lincoln's wife, Mary Todd Lincoln, was too distraught to travel with the funeral train or even to attend her husband's first funeral in the White House.

★ A near-riot broke out in Philadelphia, as crowds swarmed Independence Hall for a last look at the president.

★ The largest outpouring took place in New York City, where approximately a million spectators watched a procession of a hundred thousand march through the streets.

★ Some observers in New York climbed to the tops of trees; others paid up to a hundred dollars for a good window view!

★ Two men who would later become presidents watched the funeral processions in their respective cities: young Theodore Roosevelt in New York and Grover Cleveland in Buffalo.

★ Light drizzle and even heavy rain in Baltimore, Harrisburg, Cleveland, Indianapolis, and Chicago did not diminish the size of the crowds.

★ Great teams of horses, sometimes all black, sometimes all white, pulled Lincoln's hearse through the cities where funeral processions were held.

★ According to police reports at the time, there were "armies of pickpockets" among the crowds in every city.

★ The train traveled twenty miles an hour across the country but slowed down even more as it passed through small towns.

★ Almost every town along the way was marked by archways of evergreens, bonfires, flags, and an abundance of black drapery hanging from the houses.

★ Lincoln's assassin, John Wilkes Booth, was discovered in hiding and killed in a gun battle while the funeral train was en route.

★ At Lincoln's final funeral in Springfield, lilac bushes were in full bloom. One observer said, "I never smell lilacs without thinking of that day."

DATE DUE

MAR 1 2 2013

OUR

HAS